AF683659

A Conversation with Alfred E. Kahn

A Conversation with
Alfred E. Kahn

Held on April 3, 1980
at the American Enterprise Institute for Public Policy Research
Washington, D.C.

ISBN 0–8447–3396–2

Library of Congress Catalog Card No. 80–70503

AEI Studies 291

© 1980 by the American Enterprise Institute for Public Policy Research, Washington, D.C., and London. All rights reserved. No part of this publication may be used or reproduced in any manner whatsoever without permission in writing from the American Enterprise Institute except in the case of brief quotations embodied in news articles, critical articles, or reviews.

The views expressed in the publications of the American Enterprise Institute are those of the authors and do not necessarily reflect the views of the staff, advisory panels, officers, or trustees of AEI.

"American Enterprise Institute" and AEI are registered service marks of the American Enterprise Institute for Public Policy Research.

Printed in the United States of America

339.53
K122c

Preface

Since the American Enterprise Institute initiated its "Conversations" in 1975, a number of outstanding public figures, scholars, and specialists have contributed to the formation of public policy through them. Among many others, AEI has invited Senator Richard Lugar, Senator Daniel Patrick Moynihan, Lane Kirkland of the AFL–CIO, Secretary of Labor Ray Marshall, Robert Strauss, Gerald Ford, George Bush, the Reverend Jesse Jackson, Vladimir Bukovsky, John Connally, and Mayor Marion Barry of Washington, D.C.

The format for these conversations—a brief presentation, followed by discussion with members of a limited audience of AEI scholars and guests—is intended to produce a minimum of "talking at" the audience and a maximum of speaking to, and listening to, each other. The transcript of the discussion has been edited as lightly as possible to preserve its informal conversational tone.

We believe that this sort of exchange offers a perspective on the thinking of important public figures very different from that found in their prepared speeches and published writings. And, we believe, it is an excellent way to encourage the "competition of ideas" that is AEI's trademark.

WILLIAM J. BAROODY, JR.
President
American Enterprise Institute
for Public Policy Research

Introduction

The Honorable Alfred Kahn, advisor to the president on inflation, has had a long and distinguished career in academia and in public service. He was educated at New York and Yale universities and has taught at Ripon College and Cornell University. He is a prolific writer, and his works include a widely acclaimed two-volume set on regulation.* Dr. Kahn has had extensive public service as chairman of the New York State Public Service Commission (1974–1977), chairman of the U.S. Civil Aeronautics Board (1977–1978), and chairman of the U.S. Council on Wage and Price Stability and advisor to the president since October 24, 1978. In addition, Dr. Kahn is a member of the Research Advisory Committee to AEI's Center for the Study of Government Regulation and has participated in several AEI programs.

Inflation is perceived to be the nation's number one domestic problem. As Dr. Arthur Burns recently testified before the Senate, "Inflation . . . acts like a giant lottery, with the distribution of outcomes both arbitrary and perverse; prudence is penalized, improvidence rewarded." Dr. Kahn has grappled with this enormous problem for well over a year and has steered clear of the temptation to call for wage and price controls.

Through it all, Dr. Kahn has maintained good humor, despite public rumblings about an ever increasing inflation rate. Undoubtedly, Dr. Kahn has also experienced substantial opportunity costs. In a recent *Fortune* magazine article by Steven Solomon, Harry Walker, the highly successful agent for prominent speakers, is quoted as viewing Kahn as one of his favorite prospects. "With

*Alfred E. Kahn, *The Economics of Regulation: Principles and Institutions,* 2 vols. (New York: John Wiley & Sons, Inc., 1970).

Kahn, I could support my five grandchildren in Israel," he says. One suspects that when Dr. Kahn does finally choose to leave government service—and perhaps go on the lecture circuit—he will surely be missed.

JAMES C. MILLER III
American Enterprise Institute

A Conversation with Alfred E. Kahn

DR. KAHN: Instead of the talk that I have been giving for the last week or so on the president's new anti-inflation program, I am terribly tempted to begin with the talk I gave yesterday, on the subject of speaking and writing plain English. It's not only much more fun; it is also much easier for me to know what's right and what's wrong in that area.

One of the consolations of my present situation, however, is that the life expectancy for inflation czars is mercifully short—a situation that reminds me of the late Arthur Okun's reference to P.T. Barnum's prescription for keeping a lion and a lamb in the same cage: keep a plentiful reserve supply of lambs. The same rule, I fancy, applies to inflation czars.

This audience is as aware as I am of the major outlines of the intensified anti-inflation program that the president announced recently, and of the circumstances that elicited it. I refer to the acceleration not just of the producer price index (PPI) and consumer price index (CPI), but, more ominously, of the underlying rate that much more accurately reflects the dimensions of the longer-term inflation problem, free of the transient influence of short-term shocks. The acceleration of the CPI and PPI during the last fifteen months, and again within the last three months, was in very large measure a phenomenon of high energy prices and mortgage interest rates, both of which are bound in some degree to be proved temporary.

Much more worrisome is the behavior of what is left in the CPI after one removes energy, mortgage interest rates, and food—the latter, similarly, in consideration of the fact that the price of food at the farm is subject to wide short-term fluctuations. That residual rate had been running quite steadily at about 7½ percent in the first half of 1979, and 8 to 8½ percent in the latter part of the year. In the first quarter of 1980, however, it jumped to 12 percent. Similarly, wage increases, which had for most of 1979 run actually below the 1978 level, also began to speed up toward the end of last year and the beginning of this one; and with productivity behaving as badly as it has, this too has meant an acceleration in the rate of increase in our fundamental cost structure.

In addition, we witnessed in the first months of this year a virtual collapse of the bond market, which was in part a consequence of the disclosure that the federal budget for fiscal 1980 was going to produce not the $29 billion deficit that had been predicted only a short time before, but one in the low forties.

As I say, I am sure that most of this audience is familiar with the main components of the program that President Carter felt impelled to introduce. The first was his promise of a balanced budget for fiscal 1981. The fate of that rather rash prediction will depend, of course, on what happens to the economy generally. But the reductions in federal expenditures, on the order of $15 billion, that he has requested are real, and, I assure you, painful. I trust you will not be misled by the logic of the *Wall Street Journal,* which deprecated the cuts by pointing out that the revised budget estimate that the president presented at the same time showed fiscal 1981 expenditures going up by $9 billion; the $13 billion of cuts that it foresaw, it triumphantly observed, would therefore mean a net decline of only $4 billion.

I am not here to defend the specific $15 billion level, but there is a very great difference between the $9 billion increase, which was the simple consequence of inflation, and the $15 billion in cuts: those were real cuts, in real programs, and it took eight days of intensive consultation with the leaders of Congress to work them out; and the process, I assure you a second time, was painful.

One of the more amusing phenomena of the times is the widespread predictions we see daily that balancing the federal budget cannot make more than a 0.1 or 0.2 point difference in the inflation rate. Evidently a very large number of people are talking econometrics without realizing it. As you know, econometric models have consistently underpredicted inflation by several points these last several years. There was nothing in those models that predicted what happened to the bond market at the beginning of this year. I suggest, therefore, that merely grinding into those models a $15 billion or a $25 billion change in net federal expenditures and coming out with a very minuscule change in price levels is an exercise in futility. I am absolutely convinced—particularly in light of the behavior of that residual underlying inflation rate, the clear evidence of accelerating inflationary expectations, the sharp increase in the demand for credit, and the emergence of what appears to be a great deal of anticipatory price increasing—that we must demonstrate the ability to reduce federal spending; whether $15 billion is enough or not is something we can discuss. In any event, the importance of the cuts is simply not adequately reflected in the models that produce the familiar predictions, particularly from organized labor, that it will make a difference of only 0.1 or 0.2 of a point.

If you think you are going to catch me discussing the recent changes in credit policy in Arthur Burns's presence, you are crazy. I will observe only that, at the moment, we are taking a terrible beating on the height of interest rates and that recent experience clearly demonstrates that those high rates are the inescapable consequence of inflation. The only way of trying to prevent them, given the insistent demand for credit, would be to gin up the money supply—which would be simply self-defeating, because the more that is done, the more the demand for credit would increase.

Everything else that the president announced really constitutes an effort to take some of the burden off monetary policy. Nobody can predict that those other steps will cause interest rates miraculously to decline, but they will clearly work in that direction.

The so-called gasoline conservation fee had several virtues. First, it was something the president could do without waiting for Congress. Second, however small the additional effect, it will clearly operate to conserve gasoline. The consumption of petroleum now is about 10 percent below the 1978 level. This will help; that is all one can say. In a couple of years, if 0.5 is a reasonable prediction of long-range elasticity, it does mean 250,000 barrels less a day. The conservation fee has the other virtue of providing an insurance fund on the promise of balancing the budget. It carries a corresponding danger that Congress may, therefore, want to tap it and go lighter on cutting expenditures. I am reluctant to essay political predictions, but I sat through days of continual meetings with the congressmen and can perhaps shed some light on the likelihood of that happening. In the initial days there was a good deal of temptation to ask for higher taxes—on alcohol or on tobacco or a surcharge on high incomes. By the third day, however, that kind of prescription had simply disappeared from the conversation. It was clear to everybody that balancing the budget would not do the job unless it was accomplished by cuts in expenditures. So far, Representative Robert Giaimo and Senator Edmund Muskie have been fulfilling that undertaking.

The president went lightly over the fourth part of his announcement, which had to do with the longer-range measures that will have to be taken. The question of whether to introduce accelerated depreciation, for example, is a question probably only about timing. In the few weeks before the president's message, members of the administration had met frequently with business people who have, of course, been very strong advocates of that kind of incentive. A majority suggested waiting before proposing it to Congress, rather than in any way jeopardizing the persuasiveness of the promise to balance the budget.

In any case, the president fully recognized in his speech the importance of improved investment incentives. He also devoted more attention in his written speech than in the one he delivered to such structural reforms as trucking deregulation, communications deregulation, and banking law reform.

JAMES C. MILLER III, American Enterprise Institute: On purpose?

DR. KAHN: I am convinced the omission—actually it was of one full page of the text—was entirely inadvertent. I know from my own experience the president's dedication to these reforms. He intervened actively at critical stages in the legislative process, to ensure that we got a good trucking bill, for example. I speak with particular conviction and enthusiasm about these efforts because of my own special interest in them. I think the chances are excellent that we will get a genuine liberalization of trucking regulation. I am spending many hours trying to put together—rather, to put together again—the humpty-dumpty of communications deregulation, substantial deregulation. Suddenly, again, we have made progress on the railroad bill; and I have already alluded to the banking bill with its provision for phasing out Regulation Q. Again, Senator Abraham Ribicoff is optimistic about the possibility of our passing the Regulatory Reform Act, which has, among its provisions, not only procedural improvements, but also a general requirement that regulatory agencies apply cost-effectiveness tests.

I do not suggest that these regulatory reforms will by themselves turn the inflation rate around; I concede freely that we are using inflation as a pretext for getting some micro-improvements that would in any event be highly desirable. I do, however, disagree strongly with the economists who, regarding monopoly or cartelization as only static phenomena, contend that reforms such as these will produce only a one-shot improvement in the price level. Nonsense. It will introduce intensified pressures for improvements in efficiency, the results of which will be both continuous and incalculable. Just compare, for example, what has happened to airline fares with what has happened to the price of a bundle of inputs into the provision of airline services. The benefits of introducing competition are clearly dynamic as well as static.

Again, the president did not refer to such events of the preceding few weeks as the decision of the Commerce Department to turn down a petition by domestic growers alleging dumping of Mexican tomatoes or his decisions not to have acreage set-asides for corn or other feed grains and to drop steel trigger prices. These were no small achievements.

ARTHUR BURNS, American Enterprise Institute: When was that done?

DR. KAHN: In the last two or three weeks.

DR. BURNS: And was there an outcry from the industry, or did the manufacturers accept the decision because the trigger price mechanism was not doing much for them?

DR. KAHN: They were dissatisfied with the amount of protection it was giving them, but they did not want it dropped. It was doing enough for them to be very upset, and for Charles Schultze to have been called on the carpet yesterday by the steel caucus, and for loud interventions from the European Community, which threatened retaliation because, of course, the limitation on price competition that the trigger price mechanism provided was attractive to foreign as well as domestic producers. Every time I talk about something, I see somebody around the table who knows more about it than I do.

ROBERT W. CRANDALL, Brookings Institution: Why did Secretary of Commerce Klutznick say yesterday that you suspended it, that you didn't drop it?

DR. KAHN: I do not know the answer to that, except that I suppose he wanted to keep alive the possibility of restoring trigger prices if that seemed a less undesirable alternative to a successful series of antidumping suits: please remember, our antidumping law is a very bad one.

There are other items on my list of anti-inflationary actions by the administration during the last several weeks. One would be the president's recent rejection of the International Trade Commission's recommendation that he impose quotas on imports of leather clothing; another, his rejection also of quotas on automobile imports—a small atonement for Chrysler. In addition, it was only a few weeks ago that we persuaded the president to withdraw the two-cents-a-pound duty on imported sugar that it was in his discretion to change.

Let me turn, finally and briefly, to the pay and price standards. The administration is determined to avoid mandatory controls. The president has told all the congressmen, in four separate meetings at the White House, that he does not want the authority to impose them, that he will not ask for it, and that if a bill is passed giving him the authority, he will veto it. It is, however, urgent that we prevent as best we can workers' attempts to negotiate pay increases that would restore their pre-1979 beef and gasoline standards of living and the ability to buy new houses (even if they are not in the market for new houses). I am referring here to a deficiency in the CPI with which I think you are all acquainted.

We must also do everything we can to strengthen the credibility of the price program for two reasons: first, because we seem to be facing a wave of anticipatory price increases, and, second, because it is politically not possible to enforce the wage standards without also doing what we can to restrain price increases as well. I do not have any apologies for the intensified price jawboning that the president has instructed us to conduct, even though it is not particularly congenial to me personally. On the other hand, I have no intellectual reservations at all about trying to influence wage settlements. I cannot believe anybody believes that if we succeeded in holding the Teamsters' settlement a point or two below what it would otherwise have been—and I believe we did—then that meant we held those wages below the equilibrium, market-clearing level—as a result of which we would have caused a shortage of Teamsters. Would that we had!

I hope it is not impolite to remind this audience that Arthur Burns made one of the earliest arguments about the necessity for some kind of incomes policy, in a series of lectures that he delivered at Fordham University some twenty-five years ago.

So, as part of our intensified anti-inflationary effort, we are increasing the monitoring staff; we will try to make ourselves more visible; and we will try to jawbone Ford into some corrective action to offset the settlement by the United Auto Workers (UAW) and to jawbone Mobil Oil on its violation.

Of course, wage and price controls, whether voluntary or mandatory or something in between, do not represent a fundamental solution to the problem of inflation. That is why I place so much greater emphasis—and invest so much more enthusiasm—on structural reform. The problem of containing the painful inflation we have been experiencing in hospital costs provides an interesting illustration of this point. I had a very fruitful meeting last week with twenty-five leaders of the health care industry, which the president attended briefly. The health care industry does not like hospital cost containment—which would simply set an arithmetical limit on the permissible increases in total hospital expenditures each year—and I must admit that that approach involves a great number of problems. It would clearly be preferable to find some structural reform to put limits on the inflation of medical costs, which has resulted largely from the fact that the supply of medical services is not subject to the ordinary economic checks. In the airline industry, we were able to place very effective limits on service inflation by introducing price competition. The health industry people with whom I met all felt strongly that the administration ought to try to get together on the bills to encourage price competition in health care that are now before Congress. The week before that meeting I had testified in favor of the general principles in the Durenberger bill, which would, as a condition for exempting from employees' taxable income their contributions to health plans, require that all employers provide a choice of plans for workers, with equal contributions to each, and, to ensure a real neutrality in the choice among plans, would provide that worker's pocket, in rebates, the difference between the cost of the plans they chose and the standard employer contribution.

This is not the only possible approach to structural reform. For example, just two weeks ago, I had a talk with Governor Robert Graham of Florida, who is trying to encourage local efforts by businessmen in the Miami area to develop alternative methods of providing and financing medical care similar to what has happened in Minneapolis, to what Kaiser-Permanente has done out on the West Coast, and to what the automobile companies and the UAW are doing in Detroit. The governor's people were hoping to enlist Eastern Airlines, which is the biggest employer in that area, and thought it might be helpful if I explained to Frank Borman what they were trying to do. In view of Frank's conversion to airline deregulation, I knew that he would be receptive to a suggestion of a private, nonregulatory approach, in which the interested, private parties, with millions and millions of dollars at stake, attempted to encourage the development of alternative kinds of suppliers—health maintenance organizations and other forms of prepaid group practices—that would have incentives to control costs, which are now lacking. I was not surprised that he responded enthusiastically.

I apologize for making this account such a personal one; I hope, however, that it conveys some sense of the breadth of what we see as the necessary attack on the inflation problem.

ROBERT HELMS, American Enterprise Institute: I deal with health policy at AEI. Considering the positions that are being taken by that other agency in the administration that deals with health, aren't you taking a minority position within the administration? I am tremendously encouraged that you are making this case.

DR. KAHN: I have been making it for a long time. I feel a little bit the way I felt when I put out my style memorandum, and some of the lawyers at the Civil Aeronautics Board (CAB) grumbled. One anonymous lawyer was quoted in the paper as remarking that I had neglected to say anything about "supra" and "infra," to which I responded, "Rome was not destroyed in a day." That observation applies, in many ways, also, to the Department of Health and Human Services.

But I believe we are making progress. It will take persistence; it will take a willingness on our part to appeal to the president. But, fortunately, the president is a very strong proponent of competition, so I expect in the end to win. Let me make a rash prediction. Just as I am prepared to predict that a good trucking bill will pass Congress this session, I am prepared to offer even money that in the next few months, the administration will take a position on the principles in the Durenberger and Ullman bills, and then push for them.

ANNE BRUNSDALE, American Enterprise Institute: Do you mean a bill other than the administration's bill, such as the Durenberger bill?

DR. KAHN: Well, that is one of the problems. Some features of the Durenberger bill are in the administration's National Health Plan. A plausible case can be made for keeping the two together—that is to say, for trying to enact the structural reforms as part of the broader health plan bill. During the past year, however, the counter argument I have been encountering is that any attempt to get a competitive bill alone might destroy the delicate coalition that will get us hospital cost containment. I confess I am much less patient with that argument, when it seems to me we do have two clear opportunities to achieve some structural reform: one, by supporting a bill that would at least make the tax provision neutral; and, second, by working in the localities with business, labor, and public coalitions. I have had meetings with numerous business groups; and I have enlisted people like Clark Havighurst and Walter McClure, who is an enthusiast for the competitive approach, like Alain Enthoven, and for working with local coalitions. There is no reason why we cannot pursue both, and we will, but I do not promise success overnight. There are bases for believing that we can make some progress. I will do my best.

DR. HELMS: As you know, some of those plans were rejected earlier in the administration when there was a big push to get those ideas in.

DR. KAHN: I really cannot say any more. I do not mean that I have a lot of secret information that I am not disclosing: all I can say is I have some basis for hope.

DR. HELMS: Well, I like to take the optimistic viewpoint.

DR. KAHN: Any time any of you thinks of ways to push me or help me, I would like to know. I do have a pulpit—sometimes to be used publicly and sometimes to be used privately.

DR. BURNS: I have been following your activities for many years with a sense of great admiration, and I think that our country is under a heavy debt to you for what you have done, particularly in the field of regulation. You have fought very hard to reduce regulatory burdens, and you have had some notable successes. Now I would like to have you comment, if you will, on the president's speech of March 14. There were several elements in that speech that I thought, rightly or wrongly, would add to the regulatory burden significantly. First, the oil import fee, which I believe involves a new, complex system of entitlements; second, the revised price standards, which involve more reporting and prenotification on the part of large firms; and third—and here at least I think I know what I am talking about—the new credit restraints, which involve very heavy burdens, not only on commercial banks, but on other financial institutions and on retailers as well. I am really interested in your overall assessment; you have been a student of this problem, you bring enthusiasm to it.

DR. KAHN: Diminishing.

DR. BURNS: No, I do not think so, you are still very vigorous and enthusiastic about deregulation. I have the feeling that we were moving toward deregulation. I also have a feeling that under the March 14 pronouncement, while the president's rhetoric on the subject was good and sound, several of the proposals that I just mentioned will add heavily to the regulatory burden. Am I right or wrong? Your opinion would be worth a great deal.

DR. KAHN: That is a perfectly reasonable question, and its underlying premise is correct: every one of these steps involves some additional regulatory burdens. In the case of the oil import fee, it is not so much the burden of reporting and so on; it is the use of the entitlement system to compensate importers and place the burden of a fee on the cost of refining gasoline. But we already have an entitlement system anyhow, as the inescapable consequence of regulating the domestic price of crude oil: every refiner who uses domestic crude oil has in any event to buy entitlements, the proceeds of which go to refiners of imported oil, in order to equalize their acquisition costs. The use of that system, as the president now proposes, to convert the import fee into an excise tax on gasoline does not, I do not think, involve any additional interference. I genuinely cannot say how heavy the additional burden of red tape or paperwork is. I suspect, however, that it will be small or close to zero, because entitlements exist anyhow.

DR. BURNS: I cannot say that I understand it, but I got the impression from the press that a new entitlement program has been imposed on the old.

MR. CRANDALL: Not only that, but the old ones were going away. I mean deregulation was beginning.

DR. KAHN: The new entitlements will also go away. They all end under the statute in September 1981. The oil import fee can continue, but the proposed additional entitlements—which consist simply in a reimbursement of the importer by a refiner in proportion to the amount of gasoline he refines—will, as I understand it, also disappear in September 1981, along with the already existing system. It is simply a way of enabling the president to impose the equivalent of an excise tax, and, as I say, refiners buy entitlements all the time.

Let me turn now to the price prenotification proposal and the expansion of the required compliance reporting from 1,200 to something like 2,900 companies. There is no question that there is to be more reporting, by these 1,700 or so companies. To the extent that those companies are or were actively complying with the standards, however, they will be supplying the information that they would have had to compile anyhow. That conditional clause that I inserted there, of course, suggests that to the extent that they were not complying, they will have to compile information that they did not compile before. Please bear in mind, however, that we are talking about 1,700 additional companies being asked to supply short summaries of information that they would in any event have been gathering, to the extent that they were complying with the standards. For the millions of other businesses in the economy, there is no burden of reporting at all, except when and as we identify particular problem industries, in which event we ask for reports from companies smaller than our general sales cutoff of $250 million.

On the matter of prenotification of prices, many people urged us to require universal prenotification. We declined to do so, and announced the intention instead to do so only very selectively. For the time being, there is no prenotification requirement—we are still formulating the rules. The intention is to ask for prenotification only in situations where it makes sense—for only a limited sample of companies, or in problem industries, and only, for example, where a company's product is standardized.

DR. BURNS: You will have a larger staff that will try to tell you what makes sense, but of course, you can protect yourself.

DR. KAHN: I will try to protect myself. Many of the same companies that would be required to prenotify do so now. Once every three months or so, I meet with the executive vice president or the chairman of General Motors, U.S. Steel, or American Telephone and Telegraph, and less regularly with other companies, because they feel it is very important to let the administration know what they are doing. But there is probably no point in asking DuPont, which makes a zillion products, to come in. Prenotification can only work where the product is reasonably standardized. We will be examining particular problem situations where we can point out that prices in an industry show inexplicable increases. So we will ask for prenotification only in a problem situation, and where the company would presumably have in any event gone through the process of determining to its satisfaction that it would be complying with the standard before announcing those price increases. All we are asking is that in those cases they come and show us.*

*The Council on Wage and Price Stability (CWPS) later decided not to initiate a prenotification program so late in its second program year (which began November 1, 1979) and asked for public comments on whether to have such a program in its third program year and, if so, what form the program should take. *Federal Register*, July 11, 1980, p. 47078.—ED.

I am much less competent to discuss the credit restraints. I am tempted to say take it up with Paul Volcker, but of course, Paul will say take it up with the president, since it was the president who invoked the standards. I understand that the attempt to control revolving credit was made before.

DR. BURNS: It was attempted before?

DR. KAHN: I believe it was attempted with installment credit in the early 1950s, not with revolving credit.

DR. BURNS: That's right, and under legislation specifying just that.

DR. KAHN: I do not think there is any question of the president's authority to do it under the 1969 act.

DR. BURNS: There certainly is not.

DR. KAHN: Do you think there is a question?

DR. BURNS: No, that's the trouble with the legislation.

DR. KAHN: There is no disagreement there. I just do not feel competent to assess the burden imposed by the new regulation.

DR. BURNS: Let me ask you to help me rephrase my question. A number of the items you listed as progressing toward deregulation are yet to be carried out. Let's not talk about the future. Let's talk about the last two or three years. On balance, have we progressed toward deregulation or have we moved farther toward regulation? Is the regulatory burden increasing, or are we having crosscurrents of a sort that even you might find difficult to generalize about?

DR. KAHN: I do find it difficult to generalize. Of course there are crosscurrents, but the movement toward deregulation or toward requiring cost effectiveness is strong. The interventions by the administration on surface mining may have been insufficient, but they were sufficient to create a great storm, to take the administration into court, and to produce clear improvements. The interventions on ozone were inadequate, obviously, and yet they produced some improvement in the standard that was set and, even more important, the commissioning of new scientific studies whose results will have to be taken into account within two years, before these regulations impose significant costs on the economy.

HERBERT STEIN, American Enterprise Institute: You are talking about resisting a trend that would have gone faster without you, but that's not to say that the trend has not been in the direction of more regulation. It seems to me that the regulations imposed in the energy area alone since 1977 have a pervasiveness that must dwarf, by comparison, the cases of deregulation in the same period.

DR. KAHN: Which regulations trouble you particularly in the energy field, the various tax credits?

DR. STEIN: No, the regulations that bother me most are the requirements to shift from this source of fuel to that source of fuel, the requirements to seek permission to use a certain kind of energy. I am concerned mainly about the things that are called conservation and conversion.

DR. KAHN: Let's look at a few of those. The president deregulated crude oil, and that was no small accomplishment. It seems to me to be enormously important both politically and economically. Natural gas deregulation is proceeding gradually, albeit with an irrational accompanying effort to tilt it away from residential uses; still, there is a clear time path, a clear movement, which I think is irreversible. These price deregulations will clearly be the most powerful forces operating in the direction of economically efficient conservation and conversion, and they will make the other interventions progressively superfluous.

DR. STEIN: I do not think Dr. Burns takes issue with what has happened in the Carter administration, but with the historical trend. I would agree that the Nixon administration made some very bad decisions in 1973 and 1974; I would only complain that they have not been reversed sufficiently rapidly. But I think the whole picture, including things we have gotten into as a consequence of energy, to say nothing of regulation by the Environmental Protection Agency (EPA) and the Occupational Safety and Health Administration (OSHA), must show much more regulation now than existed six years ago.

DR. KAHN: I do not know the answer. Maybe Murray Weidenbaum is in a position to answer what the net direction is. All I can do is identify the important crosscurrents. My impression is that in the energy field, the deregulation of crude oil and natural gas outweighs what has been going the other way. But the environmental area, with the Clean Air Act and the Clean Water Act, may be another matter.

MURRAY E. WEIDENBAUM, American Enterprise Institute: I guess we are trying to say, as sincerely as we can, that we really think you are on the side of the angels. The generic carcinogenic standard clearly far outweighs in impact whatever cost savings will result in eliminating the eight hundred Mickey Mouse regulations.

DR. KAHN: Let me take the case of carcinogens. First of all, carcinogens are not to be sneezed at: I apologize for the mixed metaphor. Second, there were five different agencies with authority to move on carcinogens, and, like economists, they were all moving in their own directions. The Regulatory Council, whose establishment was widely sneered at—I confess I was skeptical about it myself—recognized the necessity of developing some common approach to the scientific assessment of carcinogens and of introducing some order of priority, in terms of their respective risks, in moving against them. The policy statement that emerged was, I submit, a very reasonable one, in which the five agencies agreed to move against the carcinogens that looked most dangerous, and move only cautiously down the list. Since I am not prepared to suggest we do nothing about carcinogens, it seems to me that represents a major accomplishment.

DR. BURNS: How does the Regulatory Council function? That is, not who is a member of it officially, but how does it function in practice?

DR. KAHN: Since I deal with the council mainly through my extremely able deputy, Ron Lewis, my direct knowledge of it is limited. First, it is responsible for the regulatory calendar.

DR. BURNS: Who is responsible: I mean not just those who are named by the president, but who does the work and attends the meetings?

DR. KAHN: I think it is primarily Douglas Costle and a staff headed by Peter Petkas.

JOSH GOTBAUM, executive assistant to Alfred Kahn: It is a small staff run largely by detailees from other agencies, principally EPA. I am almost as much in the dark as you are, but my guess is there are probably five, no more than ten professionals, whose job I would characterize as knocking regulatory agencies' heads together; but it is not a large staff.*

DR. KAHN: Under Doug Costle, that staff puts out the regulatory calendar. The calendar is not simply a listing of major regulations that are ahead; it also includes a brief discussion of the expected economic effects of each. This exercise should help improve the adequacy of regulatory analyses done by the agencies in complying with Executive Order 12044. Initially, the regulatory analyses varied considerably in their quality. EPA did very good ones—it has some really first-rate economists; but the Department of Energy put out some assessments that were abysmally bad, and other agencies were in between. I remember that Charlie Schultze, Stu Eizenstat, and I, when the effort was not moving well enough, asked the president to issue some stern instructions requesting the best possible regulatory analyses and a demonstration that the agency had selected the least costly methods. The Office of Management and Budget and the Regulatory Analysis Review Group (RARG), with Council of Economic Advisers (CEA) and CWPS staff, are responsible for policing that, and the Regulatory Council now helps spur the agencies to do a better job.

Second, the Regulatory Council has undertaken reviews of whole congeries of regulations that affect particular industries. The problem often is that the regulating right hand does not know what the left hand—not to mention the six, seven, or eight other hands—is doing. It becomes necessary to ask what is happening in the automobile industry or the steel industry, in both of which we have been mounting a particular effort because of their particular tribulations. There, with the help of the Regulatory Council, we in the Executive Office of the President have been looking at the whole range of regulatory issues and then working with the individual agencies to see which of them may be said to be cost effective and which may not. EPA took the main initiative in pushing the bubble policy—an exercise in elementary economics that tries to afford businessmen the opportunity to equalize the marginal cost of abating pollution from various sources, instead of requiring that it be done equally on every single machine and every single process. So the second thing the council is doing is looking at the whole complex of regulations affecting particular industries and trying to get some priority rating, so that everything is not required at once.

*Although the Regulatory Council started with a small group of detailees, it now has its own budget and twenty-six staff positions.—ED.

Third, it is trying to get a better scientific grasp on the problems that we now have either by themselves or by commissioning studies by the National Academy of Sciences. That's true in the carcinogen field. It is now commissioning similar studies on diesel engines, which are the subject of sometimes conflicting social objectives and regulations involving air quality and health, on the one side, and fuel economy, on the other. Somebody must look at those objectives together and weigh them one against another. As part of this assessment, the National Academy of Sciences is doing a study on the future of the diesel engine. I am not sure whether that was commissioned by the Regulatory Council or by yet another group within the administration, with representatives from the main economic and domestic policy agencies, and with Frank Press, the scientific advisor to the president, very prominently engaged.

That is about the limit of what I can say about the council. It is an attempt to introduce into the regulatory process integration and rationality, both economic and scientific, which means the setting of priorities, and the knocking of heads together to see that the regulatory agencies, pressed by the council, on one side, and by RARG, on the other, follow the lead of the president.

JACK A. MEYER, American Enterprise Institute: I would like to throw out a few sentences expressing my view of where the wage-price guidelines program is today. It seems to me that what exists now is a kind of nonprogram under the guise of a program. It has the appearance of a program, in that there is an elaborate set of rules, regulations, exceptions procedures, and so on. And yet there is very little in the way of enforcement. In fact, the companies are listed as in noncompliance, but not much happens; unions are chided for being above the guideline, but there is no real enforcement. I guess I have mixed feelings about that. On the one hand, I find the current contradiction a little bit dangerous, in the sense that I think that the administration's actions here, in putting out what is potentially the ultimate regulatory program, belie its commitment to deregulation. But at the same time, I am somewhat concerned that the administration might be making a nonprogram into a program, and that might be just as bad. I am wondering if there is not a possible danger, in terms of public cynicism, in having these elaborate rules but no real backup.

DR. MILLER: Let me amplify by pointing out that Dr. Stein recently recommended to the Joint Economic Committee that the Council on

Wage and Price Stability simply be allowed to expire, and he was joined in the recommendation by Alan Greenspan. I think . . .

DR. MEYER: I did not myself mean to suggest that, but I meant to ask whether you see some danger of public cynicism toward the credibility of government in these kinds of contradictions.

DR. KAHN: I will not be able to respond to either point adequately. I have no personal stake in refuting what Herb Stein has said. I said it would be the measure of my success at the CAB that there be nothing there when I left. Most people that I have read who have attempted to assess the program and its possible effectiveness in the first year have concluded that the wage-price guidelines did have some restraining effect. Since I just disparaged econometric models, I am not now going to hide behind Charlie Schultze's one to one and a half percentage points wage estimate. The major wage settlements in the first program year were, at least three out of four of them, one to two percentage points per year less, under any reasonable evaluation of their provisions, than the ones three years before. In the first year employers all over the country used the 7 percent guideline as a justification for holding firm. I see a great deal of compliance; and it is awfully difficult to believe—just as in running a public utilities commission—that all the sound and fury really does nothing. Had I not been chairman of the New York State Public Service Commission, major residential consumers on Long Island, who used to pay a uniform six cents a kilowatt hour, no matter when they consumed their electricity, would not now pay two and a half cents at night and thirty cents in the summer when the temperature goes above 84 degrees. I think I did that. At least, I helped.

And I think the wage-price standards have had some effect. The program was never set up for an overheated economy. The expectation was that some slack would develop in the economy, allowing us to concentrate, with the help of weakening demand, on the areas in which there is some discretion in the setting of prices and in the setting of wages. In those areas there is generally enormous attention paid to the standards, and a great feeling on the part of businessmen that they do not want to be cited as out of compliance. How does it all add up? Will I be happy to have it done? Of course, I'll be happy to have it done, but don't tell me that those are perfectly functioning markets, because they aren't.

DR. STEIN: I would like to hear how we will get the inflation rate down over the next four or five years. The president has said, correctly of course, that we will not get it down quickly, that there is a long-term problem, but he has given very little picture of what his program is beyond fiscal 1981. I contrast this picture with the recent economic messages put out in Great Britain, where there is a four-year budget plan, a four-year monetary plan, a kind of firm commitment. I cannot see what the path of the economy is, what the prospects are for the economy. Are we going to live throughout this period with these guidelines? How are we going to get out of this?

DR. KAHN: That is a challenging and useful question. I wish I had had time in the last year and a half to have thought enough about it to have a satisfactory answer. First, I do periodically, every four months, write a memo to the president about a long-run anti-inflationary strategy. The president disclosed this morning that he prays several times a day. That is as good as asking his economists for advice.

Second, I do not know much that is better than curtailing the real growth of federal expenditures; the CEA has supplied me with the following figures for the average annual rates of growth of nondefense federal expenditures in real terms, during the 1960s and 1970s, which show a dramatic reduction in the last four years: the numbers are something like 5.6, 5.4, and 5.5 percent in the first three quinquennia of the two decades, and only 0.9 percent in the period 1977 to 1981.

Third, one's set of long-term anti-inflation measures must include restraint on a continuing basis in the growth of the money supply, constant efforts to restore and strengthen the discipline of the competitive market, and wide-ranging efforts to relieve us of dependence on the Middle East and the OPEC cartel. Incidentally, there is a real short-run prospect that, partly because of the curtailment of consumption (demand is, as you know, always more elastic than the man in the street thinks) we will, during the next year, see only much more moderate increases in oil prices. This, along with the evidence of a weakening economy, which will knock out some of those silly three or four points in the CPI that are the result of mortgage interest rates, offers a clear prospect that the inflation rate will slow down from its present 18 to 20 percent rate to a still excessively high 10 percent or 11 percent underlying rate—which is labor costs *cum* productivity.

That, of course, brings us back to face the longer-run problem, from which, I realize, I have strayed. Returning, then, to the longer-range weapons, they clearly must include the encouragement of capital formation, tax reductions of a selective kind, and the attempt to hold out as long as possible through a recession, with efforts to pinpoint relief, rather than to initiate major expenditure programs. Everybody knows that the one thing we have persistently—not we, I am innocent—underestimated is the strength of the economy. That demonstrates the futility of just ginning it up. There will be no fifty-dollars-a-head tax rebates. We must also press for freer trade and for deregulation, where it will work.

DR. WEIDENBAUM: Why is the expenditure restraint focused on 1981 and beyond and not on 1980, when inflation is here now?

DR. KAHN: Remember that the fiscal year is more than half over and that we are committed to a very substantial increase, in real terms, in defense spending. There was a rigorous attempt to identify programs that could be cut in this year's budget, and there was a good deal of talk about the difference between cutting authorizations and actually cutting spending; but this is not my area of expertise. All I can say is that the cuts are painful. I wish we could also have cut the entitlements and automatic escalations—35 million people will get 14 percent increases in their social security and other pensions on July 14. We did come back to that issue time and again in our discussions with the congressional leadership, minority and majority, and were assured, quite simply, that limiting these outlays was out of the question this year. We pointed out the importance of getting control of these transfers and automatic entitlements. Everybody agreed, in principle.

There are really two separate questions involved here. One is what index you use. We kept asking to hold the escalation to, say 100 percent of the increased cost of living, not to something like 125 percent, which is what simple applications of the CPI would do. To no avail.

The second issue has to do with the substantive programs themselves and the statutory provisions that in effect decree their indefinite expansion. All we achieved was an agreement that Congress would instruct the administration to return with recommendations on both issues in time for action in 1981, which is not an election year.

MICHAEL BALZANO, American Enterprise Institute: I would like to ask a question about trial and error regulation versus uncharted regulation. We are now moving toward a new cotton dust standard that is supposed to come down this month from OSHA. It will have a very serious impact on the costs of producing textiles, and it may wipe out a great many jobs in North Carolina and South Carolina. As bad as the implications of the projections are, the prognosis appears to be bad, but it is uncharted. We have never tried this before. On the other hand, the textile industry is faced with something else coming down the road with respect to flame retardants in upholstery fabric. We have already lived through the problem of pajamas that were treated with Tris. Now we will get into upholstery fabrics. Is this really a good time to be talking about flame retardants in upholstery fabrics?

DR. KAHN: I do not know the answer to that. The cotton dust regulation happens to have been a fight that was fought out before I joined the administration. I simply do not know about the issues surrounding flame retardancy in upholstery fabrics. Nor do I know whether this is one of the regulations we have picked out for a RARG analysis; we have picked out fifteen or twenty to look at very carefully.

MR. BALZANO: The flame retardancy question is just another problem for the textile industry. The question of the benzene standards is now before the court; the cotton dust standards are before the court; the formaldehyde problem will be coming up soon. All of these may greatly affect the fiber industry. It must be rather frightening to the textile industry, because sooner or later, the price of three T-shirts may be $4.95, but they will have been made in Japan, China, or Hong Kong, where people do not worry about dust.

DR. KAHN: The dust problem, as far as I know, is over; the flame retardancy problem I can look at.

MR. BALZANO: It is over, except the impact.

DR. KAHN: I understand. But I just do not see any rational alternative to examining the costs and benefits, both of them heavily discounted for uncertainty, in each situation.

DR. BURNS: I do not know if this is a fair question; if it is not, please just ignore it. The president put out his budget message toward the end of January; his economic message followed a day or two later. The response of the bond market, the money market, the stock market was clearly adverse. That was a matter of great concern, I am sure, to the administration as well as to the rest of the country. The president made a speech on March 14 in which he announced his new anti-inflation policy. The response once again in the several critical financial markets was adverse. Did all this come as a surprise to you? If this country is to make progress in the sphere of productivity, deregulation, and inflation, a mood of optimism somehow has to be generated in the country. It appears that as yet that mood of optimism has not been achieved. Did this come as a surprise?

DR. KAHN: No.

DR. BURNS: Did you expect a negative reaction?

DR. KAHN: No, I do not think that anybody expected an adverse reaction; you follow these things much more closely than I, Arthur. There have been some positive reactions.

DR. BURNS: Yes, in the foreign exchange markets.

DR. KAHN: Right. The prices of gold and silver have behaved pleasantly. Even copper for a while was behaving better. My point, however, is that I am no longer surprised that I cannot predict what these reactions will be. Some interest rates are apparently tapering off, but Paul Volcker, who was in our meetings constantly, made us no promises. The political people would always ask him if doing certain things would bring interest rates down. He would give an answer that I assume would be similar to one that you would give.

In many ways, I think we are in a new ball game. That is why the econometric models do not work. That is the way in which I have to answer the critics on the left who express skepticism about the desirability of balancing the budget. I have no different answer to give the skeptics on the right. The proof is in what happens next. If I knew what else could have been done that would have promised a more miraculous turnaround, without destroying the economy, I certainly would have urged it on the president. It is possible that the bill that would require balancing the budget annually, or one that would restrict federal spending to 21 percent of GNP, would have done it. I just do not know.

DR. BURNS: Let me put my question in a somewhat different way. Do you think that the markets, behaving as they did first before March 14 and then after March 14, have behaved irrationally?

DR. KAHN: I will not be satisfied with my answer, but I do not think they behaved irrationally—if only because however they behave is their own justification. I do not mean to be facetious, but anybody who sold bonds on February 1 was smart, not irrational, because enough people did it to make it rational. I am very uneasy about the people who talk about inflationary expectations and inflationary psychology and so on, becuse I do not believe that those things spring out of thin air. They have an objective basis. Part of the objective basis may well have been the fact that the Pay Advisory Committee came out with a 7½ to 9½ percent standard instead of a 7 percent standard. Part of it may have been, on the part of some people sophisticated enough to see, that the committee had recommended a 7½ percent evaluation of cost of living adjustment clauses in collective bargaining contracts, which is really outrageously low. Part of it may have been that they saw that these high costs were percolating through the economy and that the CPI and the PPI were going to remain at 18 percent for a while. Doubtless, part of it was skepticism that the president, the Congress, or the Federal Reserve were really serious in professions of determination to practice fiscal and monetary restraint.

MR. CRANDALL: How much of it might have been an admission by the administration in January that it had lost control of fiscal 1980 expenditures?

DR. KAHN: Oh, I am sure that that was a part of it, both before and after March 14. I do not think it is fair to say lost control, but . . .

MR. CRANDALL: It came as a shock to a lot of people who were watching it on the outside.

DR. KAHN: Certainly, no question. Now what were the main components of that? Partly, it was that economic assumptions changed; partly, it was the unexpectedly high interest rates, which added some billions to estimated expenditures; partly, it was the defense determination; and partly, it was reacquisition of the grain after declaration of the embargo on exports to the Soviet Union. That probably covers the main factors. The recognition of what was happening was obviously a powerful factor, and it immediately cast grave doubts on the $16½ billion deficit projected for fiscal 1981. Should it have been foreseen? I do not know the answer to that. After the fact, everything should have been foreseen.

DR. BURNS: There is something that people in government overlook, and that did not start in 1977; it has been going on as long as I can remember. Inflation certainly did upset the budgetary estimates, as you have indicated; there is no question about that. But the average American's income has not risen. Salaries go on, then there is a jump; they stay at a level for a year, sometimes longer, the price level goes up, people adjust to it. Government does not stay with its estimate of expenditures; we have not developed the habit of doing that. We do not have mechanisms for ensuring that expenditures stay within budgeted limits, and that is something that the average man or woman does not quite understand. They know what they have to do; why can't government act the same way?

DR. KAHN: Well, that is really a primarily rhetorical question. Actually, in 1979, real per capita disposable income turns out to have gone up, if one uses a reasonable deflator, like the personal consumption deflator, rather than the CPI. Of course, it went up, in part, because of increased labor force participation, but it did go up. So, the one phenomenon that we do have is that people's money incomes go up, and they do increase their expenditures. And, of course, one of the nation's economic problems has been that people have increased their expenditures more rapidly than their money income. I appreciate that, and I am not denying that there might be a more powerful effect if we succumbed to what I would call irrationality and decided to impose a flat limit on government spending, even though that would encourage all sorts of new forms of accounting and all sorts of exceptions in the event of a recession. I do not deny that possibility.

MURRAY FOSS, American Enterprise Institute: Let us say it is later in 1980, the unemployment rate has risen, employment has gone down, bankruptcies have increased, and profits have gone down. In light of your fight against inflation, what would you say to the American public?

DR. KAHN: I am hesitant to say that is a ridiculous question, but I believe you know I cannot give an intelligent answer. What can I tell you? We will be tough, as tough as we can be. We recognize how serious the underlying inflation is. We will surely be slower to react to recession than in the past. But if unemployment gets to 8½ or 9 percent, while we will be much more careful about pumping up the economy than we have been in the past, still you and I live in the real world; some antirecessionary steps may be inescapable. We will try hard not to overreact. I mentioned that if we do take such steps, we will try to do things that will help productivity. That we are determined to do. We will not react with major increases in government expenditures. We will make a much greater effort to pinpoint remedies. We may wish, at a certain point, to say that the burden of social security tax increases is intolerably great, so that maybe we ought to forestall the increase scheduled for next January 1. Maybe we should use a residual piece of the oil import fee to introduce accelerated depreciation right now. That certainly is the direction in which we will look, but beyond that I just cannot say what the pressures will be. It might be satisfying to know that those pressures are not likely to be so great before November 1980, so that what happens will not be heavily influenced by the prospect of an election. That is one benefit from the amazing strength of the American economy. How long have we been wrong about this recession?

But it is precisely our inability to predict the course of the economy in the near future that makes it impossible for me to tell you what the proper policies should be in the months immediately ahead. All I can assure you is that our policies will be heavily influenced by our recognition of how serious the threat of inflation is and of the necessity of adopting such short-term remedial policies as offer the greatest likelihood of combatting inflation over the longer run. Easier said than done, I realize.